EMMANUEL JOSEPH

Faith in the Machine, Building a Career and Family in a World of Artificial Minds

Copyright © 2025 by Emmanuel Joseph

All rights reserved. No part of this publication may be reproduced, stored or transmitted in any form or by any means, electronic, mechanical, photocopying, recording, scanning, or otherwise without written permission from the publisher. It is illegal to copy this book, post it to a website, or distribute it by any other means without permission.

First edition

This book was professionally typeset on Reedsy.
Find out more at reedsy.com

Contents

1	Chapter 1: Beginnings in a Brave New World	1
2	Chapter 2: Navigating a New Reality	3
3	Chapter 3: The Family Frontier	5
4	Chapter 4: Building Bridges	7
5	Chapter 5: Challenges and Triumphs	9
6	Chapter 6: The Role of Faith	11
7	Chapter 7: The Power of Community	13
8	Chapter 8: Innovation and Ethics	15
9	Chapter 9: Mentorship and Legacy	17
10	Chapter 10: The Changing Landscape	19
11	Chapter 11: Balancing Act	21
12	Chapter 12: The Future of AI	23
13	Chapter 13: The Global Movement	25
14	Chapter 14: Personal Growth and Reflection	27
15	Chapter 15: A Vision for the Future	29
16	Chapter 16: The Journey Continues	31

1

Chapter 1: Beginnings in a Brave New World

In the year 2025, the advent of artificial intelligence (AI) had irrevocably transformed the world. Jobs were being redefined, and the concept of career paths was undergoing radical change. As society embraced AI, people had to navigate a new reality where machines were not just tools, but collaborators. For many, including Sarah, an ambitious young woman from Abuja, this shift was both daunting and exhilarating. With a passion for technology and a deep-seated desire to make a difference, Sarah embarked on a journey to build a career in AI, driven by her faith in its potential to create a better world.

Sarah's journey began with her enrolling in a prestigious university renowned for its AI research. Here, she found herself amidst a diverse group of students, each bringing their unique perspectives to the table. The curriculum was rigorous, demanding not just technical prowess but also ethical considerations. Sarah quickly realized that building a career in AI was not just about mastering algorithms, but about understanding the societal impact of these technologies. Her professors emphasized the importance of developing AI systems that were fair, transparent, and beneficial to all.

As Sarah delved deeper into her studies, she encountered various challenges that tested her resolve. The field was highly competitive, and the pace of technological advancements was relentless. However, her determination never wavered. She sought mentorship from leading experts and participated in cutting-edge research projects. These experiences enriched her understanding and fueled her passion. Sarah's commitment to ethical AI became a guiding principle, shaping her vision for the future.

In the final year of her studies, Sarah was presented with an opportunity that would shape the course of her career. She was offered an internship at an innovative AI startup, known for its groundbreaking work in healthcare. This was a chance to apply her knowledge in a real-world setting and make a tangible impact. With her sights set on this new horizon, Sarah embarked on the next phase of her journey, ready to contribute to the world of artificial minds.

2

Chapter 2: Navigating a New Reality

The internship at the AI startup proved to be a pivotal experience for Sarah. Immersed in a dynamic and fast-paced environment, she was exposed to the practical challenges and opportunities of AI development. The startup's mission was to leverage AI to revolutionize healthcare, aiming to improve patient outcomes and streamline medical processes. Sarah was assigned to a team working on a project that used machine learning algorithms to predict patient diagnoses based on medical records and test results.

Working alongside seasoned professionals, Sarah quickly learned the importance of collaboration and communication. The interdisciplinary nature of the project required her to interact with data scientists, software engineers, and medical experts. Each team member brought their unique expertise to the table, and Sarah found herself thriving in this collaborative ecosystem. Her technical skills were put to the test as she tackled complex problems and contributed innovative solutions to the project.

As the months passed, Sarah began to see the real-world impact of her work. The AI system they developed showed promising results, accurately predicting patient diagnoses and enabling doctors to provide timely and effective treatments. The success of the project validated her belief in the potential of AI to drive positive change. However, it also highlighted the ethical dilemmas and responsibilities that came with developing such powerful technologies. Sarah was keenly aware of the need for transparency, accountability, and bias mitigation in AI systems.

Outside of her work, Sarah's personal life was also evolving. She had met David, a fellow AI enthusiast, at a tech conference, and they quickly formed a strong bond. David shared Sarah's passion for technology and her commitment to ethical AI. Together, they dreamed of a future where AI would enhance human capabilities and create a more equitable society. Their relationship blossomed, providing Sarah with a sense of balance and support as she navigated the complexities of her career.

As Sarah's internship came to an end, she was offered a full-time position at the startup. This marked the beginning of a new chapter in her career, one where she could continue to innovate and make a difference. With David by her side, Sarah felt ready to face the challenges ahead. Together, they embarked on a journey to build a future where humans and machines coexisted harmoniously, driven by their shared faith in the transformative power of AI.

3

Chapter 3: The Family Frontier

As Sarah and David settled into their new life, they began to contemplate the idea of starting a family. The prospect of raising children in a world dominated by AI was both exciting and intimidating. They were determined to instill in their children the values of curiosity, empathy, and ethical responsibility. Sarah and David believed that the next generation would play a crucial role in shaping the future of AI, and they wanted to equip their children with the knowledge and skills to navigate this ever-changing landscape.

The couple's discussions often revolved around the impact of AI on various aspects of family life. They explored how AI could enhance education, healthcare, and daily routines. Smart home devices, personalized learning platforms, and AI-driven healthcare solutions were just a few examples of the potential benefits. However, they were also mindful of the challenges, such as privacy concerns, digital addiction, and the need for human connection. Balancing the advantages of AI with the importance of maintaining a healthy, human-centered lifestyle became a central theme in their family planning.

When Sarah and David welcomed their first child, they embraced the role of tech-savvy parents. They used AI-powered baby monitors to track their child's health and development, and educational apps to stimulate early learning. However, they also made a conscious effort to spend quality time with their child, engaging in activities that fostered creativity and emotional intelligence. They were determined to create an environment where their child could thrive, both in the digital and physical realms.

As their family grew, Sarah and David continued to advocate for ethical AI practices. They became involved in community initiatives and educational programs, sharing their knowledge and experiences with others. They believed that fostering a culture of ethical responsibility and critical thinking was essential for the future. By empowering their children and their community, they hoped to contribute to a world where AI was used to enhance human potential and create a more just and equitable society.

4

Chapter 4: Building Bridges

Sarah's career continued to flourish as she took on more responsibilities at the AI startup. She was now leading a team of talented professionals, working on projects that addressed pressing societal issues. One of their most ambitious initiatives was to develop AI solutions for underserved communities, focusing on areas such as education, healthcare, and economic development. Sarah's commitment to making a positive impact was stronger than ever, and she was determined to bridge the gap between technology and social good.

The team collaborated with local organizations, government agencies, and international partners to identify the needs of these communities and design tailored AI solutions. They faced numerous challenges, including limited resources, infrastructural constraints, and cultural differences. However, Sarah's leadership and vision inspired her team to persevere. They worked tirelessly to develop AI systems that were not only effective but also respectful of the unique contexts and needs of each community.

One of their most successful projects was an AI-powered educational platform designed for remote and rural areas. The platform provided personalized learning experiences, adapting to each student's abilities and progress. It also offered resources and training for teachers, enabling them to better support their students. The impact was profound, with students achieving higher levels of academic performance and gaining access to opportunities that were previously out of reach. Sarah's heart swelled with pride as she witnessed the transformative power of AI in action.

Beyond her professional achievements, Sarah remained deeply committed to her family. She and David continued to nurture their children's growth, encouraging them to explore their interests and develop their talents. They instilled in them the importance of empathy, integrity, and a sense of social responsibility. Sarah believed that by raising compassionate and conscientious individuals, they could help shape a future where AI was used for the greater good.

5

Chapter 5: Challenges and Triumphs

As Sarah's career progressed, she encountered various challenges that tested her resilience and adaptability. The rapidly evolving AI landscape meant that she had to stay ahead of the curve, continuously learning and updating her skills. New ethical dilemmas emerged as AI technologies became more sophisticated and pervasive. The pressure to deliver innovative solutions while maintaining ethical standards was immense, but Sarah remained steadfast in her commitment to doing what was right.

One of the most significant challenges Sarah faced was the increasing scrutiny and skepticism surrounding AI. Public concerns about job displacement, privacy, and the potential misuse of AI technologies were growing. Sarah recognized the need for transparency and open dialogue to address these fears and build trust. She became an advocate for responsible AI development, speaking at conferences, participating in panel discussions, and engaging with policymakers. Her efforts to bridge the gap between technologists and the public were instrumental in fostering a more informed and inclusive conversation about AI.

Despite the challenges, Sarah also experienced numerous triumphs that validated her faith in the power of AI. Her team successfully launched several projects that had a meaningful impact on people's lives. From improving access to healthcare in remote areas to creating job opportunities through

AI-driven entrepreneurship programs, their work made a tangible difference. Sarah's dedication and leadership were recognized with numerous awards and accolades, but what mattered most to her was the positive change they were creating.

On the home front, Sarah and David continued to support each other and their family. They navigated the complexities of balancing demanding careers with family life, always prioritizing their children's well-being and growth. Their shared values and strong partnership were the foundation of their success. Together, they celebrated their achievements and faced their challenges, confident in their ability to build a better future.

6

Chapter 6: The Role of Faith

Faith played a central role in Sarah's journey, guiding her through the ups and downs of her career and family life. Her belief in the potential of AI to create a better world was unwavering, even in the face of challenges and uncertainties. This faith was not blind optimism but a deep sense of purpose that guided her decisions and actions. She believed that by harnessing the power of AI responsibly and ethically, humanity could overcome some of its most pressing challenges and create a more just and equitable society.

Sarah's faith was also rooted in her spirituality and her connection to a higher power. This provided her with strength and resilience, especially during difficult times. Her spiritual beliefs helped her maintain a sense of balance and perspective, reminding her of the importance of compassion, humility, and service to others. These values were central to her approach to AI, as she sought to develop technologies that uplifted and empowered individuals and communities.

David shared Sarah's faith, and their spiritual journey was an integral part of their relationship. They supported each other in their personal and professional endeavors, drawing strength from their shared beliefs. Their faith also played a crucial role in raising their children, as they instilled in them the importance of kindness, empathy, and a sense of responsibility towards others. They taught their children to see AI as a tool for good, one that could be used to address societal issues and create a better world.

As Sarah continued to build her career and family, her faith remained a guiding force. It shaped her vision for the future and motivated her to persevere in the face of challenges. With a deep sense of purpose and a commitment to ethical AI, Sarah was determined to make a lasting impact on the world.

7

Chapter 7: The Power of Community

Sarah and David recognized the importance of community in their journey. They believed that building strong, supportive networks was essential for personal and professional growth. They actively sought out opportunities to connect with like-minded individuals and organizations, both locally and globally. Through these connections, they found inspiration, mentorship, and collaboration.

One of the key initiatives they were involved in was a local tech community that brought together AI enthusiasts, researchers, and practitioners. This community provided a platform for sharing knowledge, exchanging ideas, and fostering innovation. Sarah and David played active roles in organizing events, workshops, and hackathons, creating opportunities for others to learn and grow. They believed that by empowering individuals and nurturing talent, they could contribute to the advancement of AI in a positive and ethical manner.

In addition to their local efforts, Sarah and David were also involved in global initiatives that aimed to address pressing societal challenges. They participated in international conferences, joined task forces, and collaborated with organizations working on AI for social good. These experiences broadened their perspectives and deepened their understanding of the diverse ways AI could be used to create positive change. They were particularly passionate about projects that focused on education, healthcare, and economic development in underserved communities.

The power of community was also evident in their family life. Sarah and David emphasized the importance of building strong relationships with their neighbors, friends, and extended family. They believed that a supportive and interconnected community was vital for their children's well-being and growth. By fostering a sense of belonging and collaboration, they hoped to create a nurturing environment where everyone could thrive.

Through their involvement in various communities, Sarah and David were able to amplify their impact and contribute to a larger movement for ethical AI. They were inspired by the collective efforts of individuals and organizations working towards a common goal, and they were proud to be part of a global community dedicated to making the world a better place.

8

Chapter 8: Innovation and Ethics

Innovation was at the heart of Sarah's work in AI, but she always approached it with a strong ethical compass. She believed that technological advancements should be guided by principles of fairness, transparency, and accountability. Throughout her career, she advocated for the development of AI systems that prioritized human well-being and respected individual rights.

One of the key projects that exemplified Sarah's commitment to ethical innovation was the development of an AI-powered healthcare platform. This platform aimed to improve access to healthcare services in remote and underserved areas. By leveraging AI, the platform could analyze medical data, provide personalized treatment recommendations, and facilitate remote consultations with healthcare professionals. The goal was to bridge the gap between urban and rural healthcare and ensure that everyone had access to quality medical care.

However, the project also raised important ethical considerations. Sarah and her team were keenly aware of the potential risks associated with AI in healthcare, such as data privacy, algorithmic bias, and the need for informed consent. They worked diligently to address these concerns, implementing robust data protection measures, conducting thorough bias assessments, and ensuring that patients were fully informed about how their data would be used. The team's commitment to ethical practices earned them recognition and trust from both the medical community and the public.

In addition to her professional work, Sarah also contributed to the broader discourse on AI ethics. She published articles, gave talks, and participated in panel discussions on the responsible use of AI. Her insights were informed by her practical experience and her deep commitment to ethical principles. She emphasized the need for ongoing dialogue and collaboration between technologists, policymakers, and society at large to ensure that AI was developed and deployed in ways that aligned with human values.

Sarah's dedication to ethical innovation extended beyond her work in healthcare. She was also involved in projects that addressed issues such as environmental sustainability, social justice, and economic inclusion. Her holistic approach to AI development was driven by a belief in the transformative potential of technology when guided by ethical principles. Through her work, Sarah demonstrated that it was possible to push the boundaries of innovation while remaining steadfast in one's commitment to doing what was right.

9

Chapter 9: Mentorship and Legacy

Mentorship was a central theme in Sarah's journey, both as a mentee and a mentor. Throughout her career, she benefited from the guidance and support of experienced professionals who shared their knowledge and wisdom with her. These mentors played a crucial role in shaping her career, helping her navigate challenges, and providing valuable insights that informed her decisions.

As Sarah's career progressed, she recognized the importance of paying it forward and becoming a mentor herself. She was passionate about nurturing the next generation of AI professionals and empowering them to pursue their goals. She actively sought out opportunities to mentor young talent, offering guidance, support, and encouragement. Through formal mentorship programs, one-on-one coaching, and informal interactions, Sarah made a lasting impact on the lives of many aspiring technologists.

One of the key lessons Sarah imparted to her mentees was the importance of ethical responsibility. She emphasized that as AI professionals, they had a duty to consider the broader implications of their work and strive to develop technologies that served the greater good. She encouraged them to approach their work with integrity, humility, and a sense of purpose, always keeping in mind the potential impact of their innovations on society.

Sarah's mentorship extended beyond technical skills and knowledge. She also focused on personal and professional development, helping her mentees build confidence, resilience, and leadership abilities. She shared her experiences, both successes and failures, to provide valuable lessons and insights. Her mentees appreciated her genuine care and dedication, and many of them went on to achieve remarkable success in their own careers.

As Sarah reflected on her journey, she felt a deep sense of fulfillment and pride in the legacy she was creating. She was proud of the positive impact she had made through her work and the relationships she had built along the way. Her commitment to ethical AI, community, and mentorship was a testament to her belief in the transformative power of technology and the importance of human values. Through her efforts, she hoped to inspire others to continue the journey towards a future where AI was a force for good.

10

Chapter 10: The Changing Landscape

The world of AI was constantly evolving, and Sarah was always at the forefront of these changes. She witnessed firsthand the rapid advancements in AI technologies and their increasing integration into various aspects of society. From autonomous vehicles to AI-driven financial systems, the possibilities seemed endless. However, with these advancements came new challenges and opportunities that required careful consideration and thoughtful action.

One of the significant changes Sarah observed was the growing role of AI in the workplace. Automation and AI-driven processes were transforming industries, creating new job opportunities while also displacing traditional roles. Sarah recognized the need for a proactive approach to address these changes, advocating for policies and initiatives that supported workforce reskilling and upskilling. She believed that by equipping individuals with the skills needed for the AI-driven economy, society could harness the benefits of automation while minimizing its negative impact.

Another key development was the increasing focus on AI ethics and governance. Governments, organizations, and academia were recognizing the importance of establishing frameworks to ensure the responsible development and deployment of AI. Sarah was actively involved in these efforts, contributing her expertise to shape policies and guidelines that promoted transparency, accountability, and fairness. She believed that a collaborative approach was essential to address the complex ethical and societal issues associated with AI.

Sarah also observed the growing importance of interdisciplinary collaboration in AI research and development. The convergence of AI with fields such as biology, psychology, and environmental science opened up new possibilities for addressing global challenges. She was particularly excited about projects that aimed to use AI to combat climate change, enhance mental health care, and promote sustainable development. By bringing together diverse perspectives and expertise, these initiatives demonstrated the potential of AI to create meaningful and lasting impact.

Despite the rapid pace of change, Sarah remained grounded in her core values and principles. She continued to advocate for the responsible and ethical use of AI, driven by her belief in its potential to improve lives and create a more equitable society. Her work was a testament to the idea that technology, when guided by human values, could be a powerful force for good.

11

Chapter 11: Balancing Act

Balancing a demanding career in AI with family life was a constant challenge for Sarah, but one she embraced wholeheartedly. She and David were committed to maintaining a healthy work-life balance, ensuring that their professional pursuits did not come at the expense of their family well-being. They believed that achieving this balance was essential for their happiness and success.

One of the strategies Sarah and David employed was setting clear boundaries between work and family time. They established routines that allowed them to dedicate quality time to their children, engage in family activities, and support each other's personal and professional goals and prioritizing self-care. They also made a conscious effort to stay present and engaged during family time, setting aside work-related distractions and focusing on nurturing their relationships.

Another key aspect of their balancing act was fostering a supportive and flexible work environment. Sarah advocated for policies that promoted work-life balance, such as remote work options, flexible schedules, and parental leave. She believed that creating a culture of support and understanding was essential for the well-being and productivity of employees. By leading by example and championing these initiatives, Sarah contributed to a positive and inclusive workplace.

In addition to their efforts at home and work, Sarah and David also prioritized their personal growth and well-being. They made time for hobbies, exercise, and self-reflection, recognizing the importance of maintaining a healthy mind and body. They supported each other in pursuing their individual interests and passions, which helped them stay energized and motivated.

Despite the challenges, Sarah and David found joy and fulfillment in their journey. They cherished the moments of connection and growth with their children, the successes and learning experiences in their careers, and the shared adventures and discoveries along the way. By prioritizing balance and well-being, they created a harmonious and rewarding life.

12

Chapter 12: The Future of AI

As Sarah looked to the future, she was filled with a sense of optimism and excitement about the potential of AI. The advancements in AI technology had the power to address some of the world's most pressing challenges and create new opportunities for innovation and growth. However, she also recognized the need for ongoing vigilance and responsibility to ensure that these technologies were developed and deployed ethically.

Sarah believed that the future of AI depended on the collective efforts of individuals, organizations, and governments. She was committed to fostering collaboration and dialogue to address the complex ethical and societal issues associated with AI. By working together, she believed that it was possible to create a future where AI was a force for good, enhancing human capabilities and promoting social justice.

One of the key areas of focus for the future was the development of AI-driven solutions for global challenges such as climate change, healthcare, and education. Sarah was particularly passionate about projects that aimed to create sustainable and equitable solutions for these issues. She believed that by leveraging AI's capabilities, it was possible to create a more just and resilient world.

As she continued her work in AI, Sarah remained dedicated to her core values of ethical responsibility, community, and mentorship. She was determined to leave a lasting legacy that inspired others to pursue their goals and make a positive impact on the world. With a deep sense of purpose and a commitment to doing what was right, Sarah looked to the future with hope and determination.

13

Chapter 13: The Global Movement

Sarah's dedication to ethical AI and her efforts to create positive change resonated with individuals and organizations around the world. She became a prominent figure in the global AI community, known for her commitment to responsible innovation and her vision for a better future. Her work inspired a global movement that sought to harness the power of AI for social good.

Through her involvement in various international initiatives, Sarah connected with like-minded individuals who shared her passion for ethical AI. She collaborated with researchers, policymakers, and activists from diverse backgrounds, working together to address the complex challenges and opportunities presented by AI. Their collective efforts led to the creation of frameworks and guidelines that promoted transparency, accountability, and fairness in AI development.

One of the key achievements of this global movement was the establishment of an international coalition dedicated to advancing ethical AI. This coalition brought together stakeholders from different sectors, including academia, industry, and civil society, to collaborate on research, policy, and advocacy. Sarah played a central role in shaping the coalition's goals and initiatives, ensuring that they aligned with her vision of a just and equitable future.

The global movement also emphasized the importance of education and awareness. Sarah and her colleagues launched campaigns and programs to educate the public about AI and its implications. They aimed to demystify AI, dispel myths, and empower individuals with the knowledge and tools to engage with AI technologies responsibly. By fostering a more informed and engaged society, they hoped to create a culture of ethical AI that prioritized human well-being and social justice.

As the global movement gained momentum, Sarah felt a deep sense of fulfillment and pride. She was inspired by the collective efforts of individuals and organizations working towards a common goal. Together, they were building a future where AI was a force for good, driven by values of compassion, integrity, and responsibility.

14

Chapter 14: Personal Growth and Reflection

Throughout her journey, Sarah experienced significant personal growth and transformation. The challenges and triumphs she encountered shaped her into a resilient and compassionate leader. She learned valuable lessons about the importance of staying true to her values, embracing change, and nurturing her relationships.

Sarah's journey was also marked by moments of reflection and introspection. She took time to pause and evaluate her experiences, considering how they aligned with her goals and aspirations. This practice of self-reflection helped her stay grounded and focused, enabling her to navigate the complexities of her career and family life with clarity and purpose.

One of the key insights Sarah gained was the importance of balance and well-being. She recognized that maintaining a healthy mind and body was essential for her personal and professional success. She prioritized self-care, engaged in activities that brought her joy, and sought support from her family and community. This holistic approach to well-being allowed her to stay energized and motivated, even in the face of challenges.

Sarah also developed a deep sense of gratitude for the people and experiences that shaped her journey. She appreciated the support of her family, the mentorship of her colleagues, and the opportunities to make a positive impact. This sense of gratitude fueled her commitment to giving back and helping others achieve their goals.

As Sarah reflected on her journey, she felt a profound sense of fulfillment and purpose. She was proud of the legacy she was creating and the positive change she was contributing to. With a deep sense of gratitude and a commitment to ethical AI, Sarah looked to the future with hope and determination, ready to continue her journey of growth and impact.

15

Chapter 15: A Vision for the Future

As Sarah's career continued to evolve, she developed a clear vision for the future of AI. She envisioned a world where AI technologies were used to enhance human capabilities, promote social justice, and address global challenges. This vision was driven by her belief in the transformative potential of AI and her commitment to ethical responsibility.

One of the key components of Sarah's vision was the creation of AI-driven solutions for sustainable development. She believed that AI had the power to address issues such as climate change, poverty, and healthcare disparities. By leveraging AI's capabilities, it was possible to create innovative solutions that promoted environmental sustainability, economic inclusion, and social equity.

Sarah was also passionate about the role of education in shaping the future of AI. She believed that empowering individuals with the knowledge and skills to engage with AI technologies was essential for creating a more informed and inclusive society. She advocated for the integration of AI ethics and literacy into educational curricula, ensuring that future generations were equipped to navigate the complexities of the AI-driven world.

Another key aspect of Sarah's vision was the importance of collaboration and interdisciplinary approaches. She believed that addressing the ethical and societal implications of AI required input from diverse perspectives and expertise. She championed initiatives that brought together technologists, policymakers, social scientists, and activists to work towards common goals. By fostering a collaborative and inclusive approach, Sarah aimed to create a future where AI was developed and deployed in ways that aligned with human values.

As Sarah pursued her vision for the future, she remained grounded in her core values of compassion, integrity, and responsibility. She was committed to making a positive impact and creating a legacy that inspired others to pursue their goals and contribute to the greater good. With a clear vision and a deep sense of purpose, Sarah looked to the future with optimism and determination.

16

Chapter 16: The Journey Continues

Sarah's journey in the world of AI was far from over. As she continued to navigate the ever-changing landscape of technology and society, she remained committed to her mission of ethical innovation and social good. She was inspired by the progress she had made and the impact she had created, but she knew that there was still much work to be done.

Sarah's experiences had equipped her with the knowledge, skills, and resilience to face new challenges and seize new opportunities. She was excited about the future possibilities and the potential for AI to create meaningful and lasting change. With a deep sense of purpose and a commitment to doing what was right, she was ready to continue her journey of growth and impact.

As she moved forward, Sarah was guided by her faith, her values, and her vision for the future. She believed that by staying true to these principles, she could make a positive difference in the world and contribute to the creation of a just and equitable society. With David by her side and the support of her family and community, she was confident in her ability to navigate the complexities of the AI-driven world and build a better future for all.

The journey of building a career and family in a world of artificial minds was challenging, but it was also deeply rewarding. Sarah's story was a testament to the power of perseverance, ethical responsibility, and the transformative potential of AI. As she continued her journey, she was filled with hope and determination, ready to embrace the future and make a lasting impact.

Faith in the Machine: Building a Career and Family in a World of Artificial Minds follows the compelling journey of Sarah, a visionary woman determined to thrive in an AI-driven world. From her early days as a passionate student to her role as a leader in ethical AI innovation, Sarah navigates the complexities of career and family with unwavering faith and a deep sense of purpose.

Set against the backdrop of rapid technological advancements, the story explores Sarah's challenges and triumphs as she builds a career in AI, advocates for responsible development, and balances the demands of work and family life. Alongside her supportive partner David, Sarah's journey is marked by her commitment to ethical responsibility, community involvement, and mentorship.

The book delves into the transformative potential of AI, highlighting its impact on various aspects of society, including healthcare, education, and economic development. Sarah's story is a testament to the power of perseverance, collaboration, and faith in creating a better future for all.

With a focus on ethical innovation and the importance of human values, **Faith in the Machine** is a thought-provoking and inspiring tale that underscores the significance of responsible AI development and the enduring strength of the human spirit.

www.ingramcontent.com/pod-product-compliance
Lightning Source LLC
LaVergne TN
LVHW020500080526
838202LV00057B/6073